Where Does the Garbage Go?

What happens to your garbage at home? Do you recycle?

Written by Cathy Torrisi • Illustrated by Pattie Silver

Hi, I'm Mr. G. I used to goof around with my gooey gum. What a mess! Now I throw my gum in the garbage can where it belongs.

Did you ever wonder where the garbage goes after we throw it away? Let's find out!

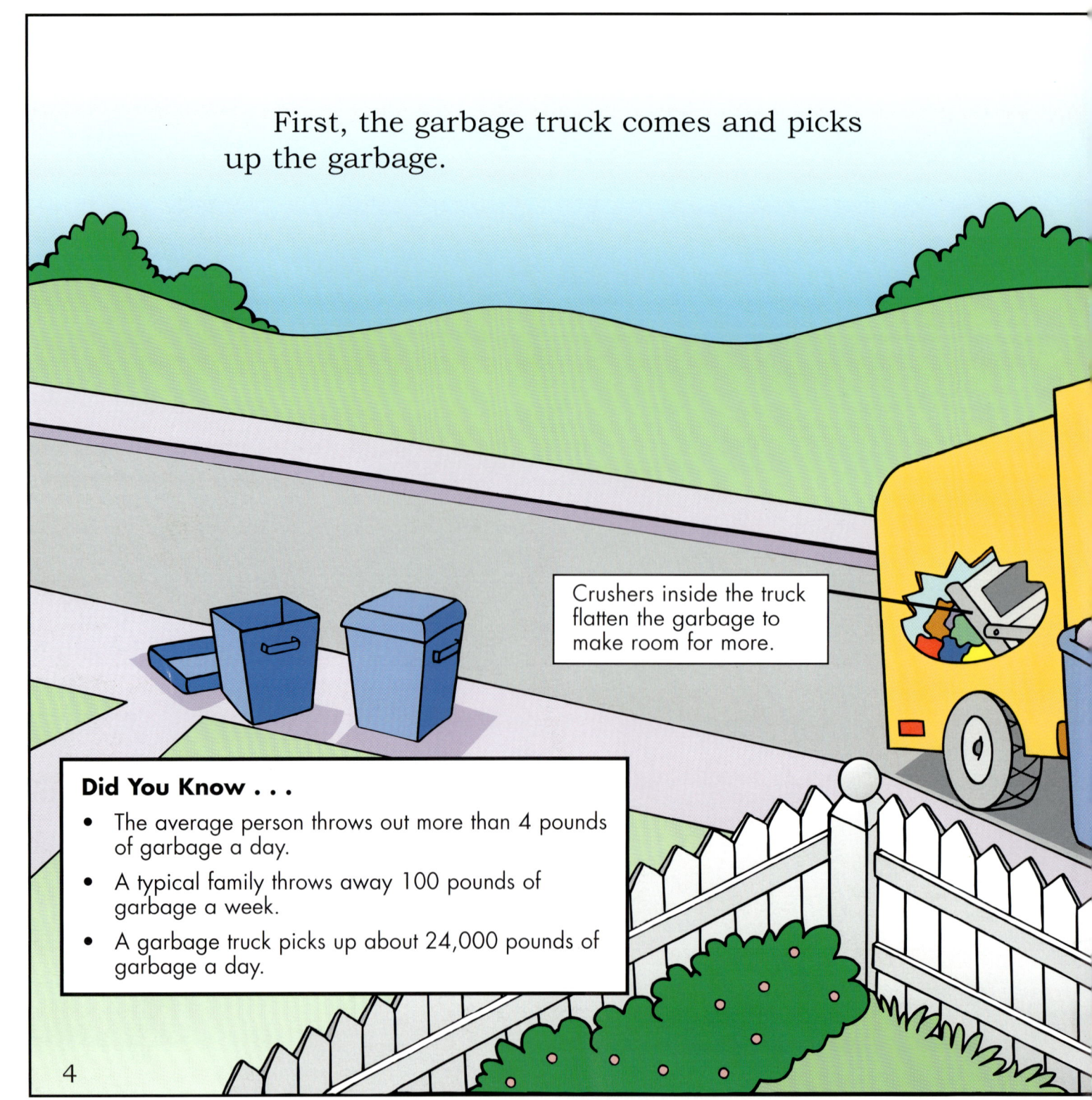

First, the garbage truck comes and picks up the garbage.

Crushers inside the truck flatten the garbage to make room for more.

Did You Know . . .
- The average person throws out more than 4 pounds of garbage a day.
- A typical family throws away 100 pounds of garbage a week.
- A garbage truck picks up about 24,000 pounds of garbage a day.

Sometimes the garbage gets burned in a huge oven called an **incinerator.** Burning garbage can make energy for electricity. But it can also make harmful smoke and ashes.

1) The garbage truck dumps the garbage onto a conveyor belt.

2) A shredder chops the garbage into small pieces.

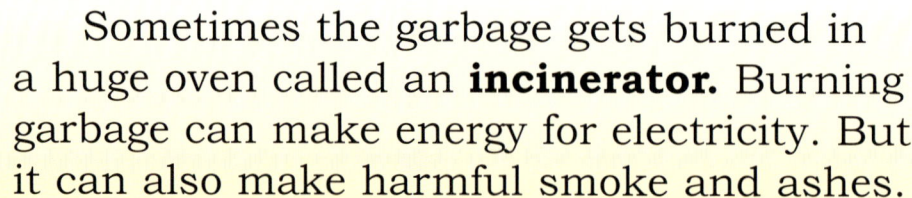

When the landfill gets full, workers cover it with a thick layer of clay or soil and a sheet of plastic. Then comes more soil. Parks, parking lots, and even ski slopes can be built on top of old landfills!

Did You Know . . .
- The world's largest landfill, in Staten Island, New York, has a mountain of garbage as high as a 20-story building! It can be seen from outer space!

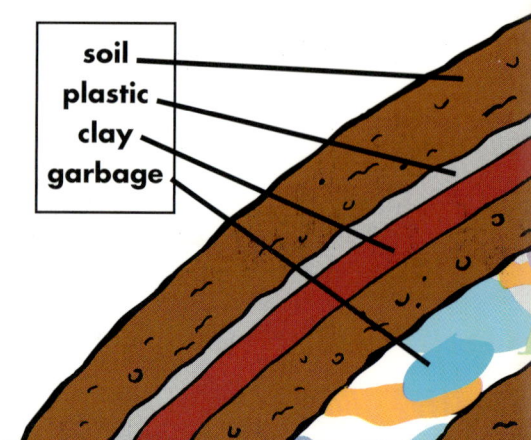

Every time a landfill closes, we have to make a new one. If we make too much garbage, we'll run out of places to put it. Then garbage will pile up everywhere!

We don't want that to happen! So what can we do?

We can use the three R's: Reduce, Reuse, Recycle!

The first R is **reduce.** That means make less trash. We can make less trash by buying things without extra packaging.

The second R is **reuse.** That means use something again or in a different way.

Turn a plastic gallon jug into a piggy bank!

Plant flowers in old yogurt containers. Make an indoor garden!

Turn old socks into great puppets!

Wrap gifts in the Sunday comics!

The third R is **recycle.** That means make something new from something old.

It's easy!

You just separate the glass, metal, paper, and plastic from your garbage. Put each one in a separate container.

In some places, a recycling truck picks up the containers and brings them to a recycling plant. In other places, you have to bring them to the recycling plant yourself.

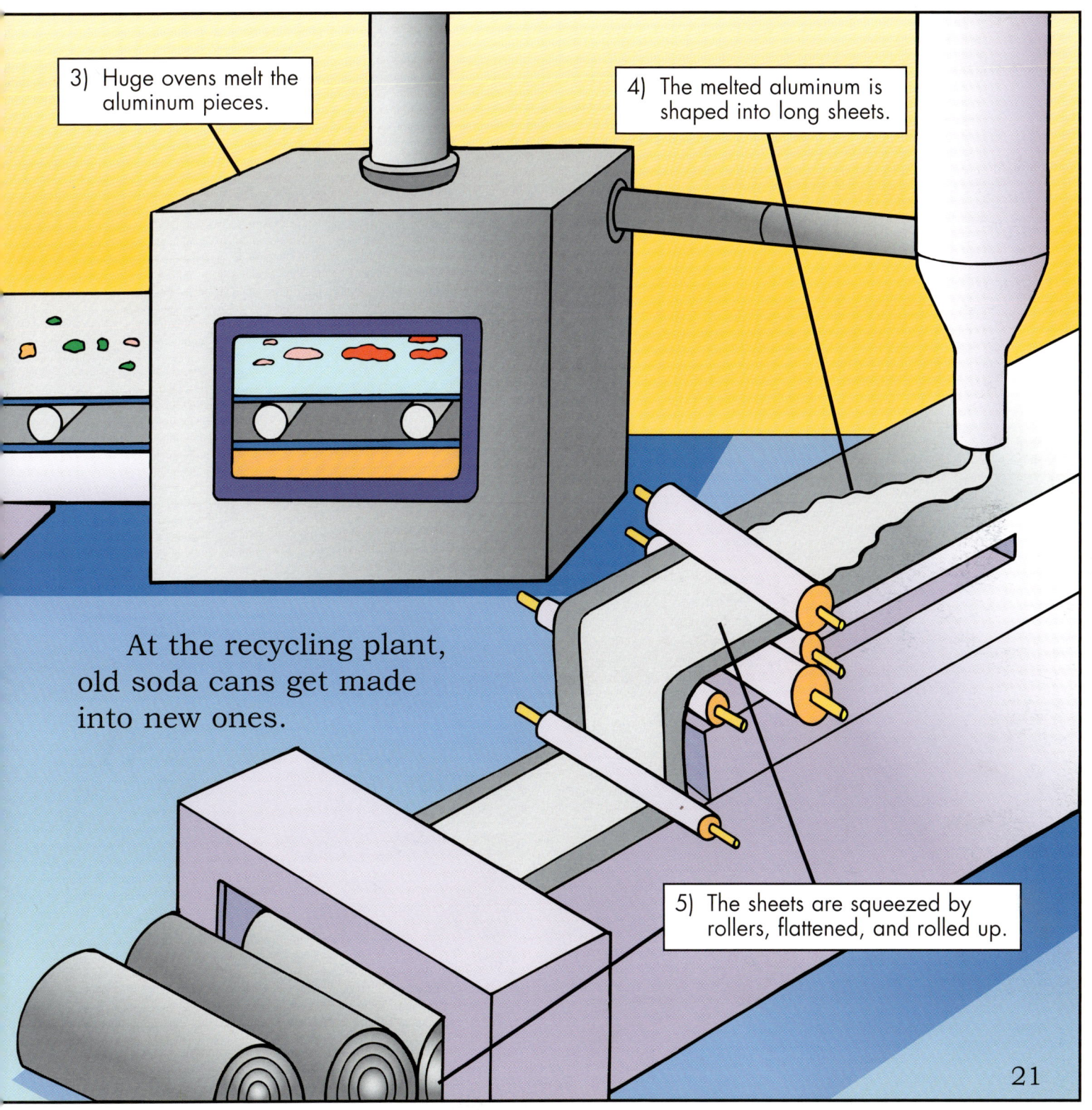

3) Huge ovens melt the aluminum pieces.

4) The melted aluminum is shaped into long sheets.

At the recycling plant, old soda cans get made into new ones.

5) The sheets are squeezed by rollers, flattened, and rolled up.

Soda cans aren't the only things you can recycle!

Old glass can be used to make new bottles and jars, windows, bathtubs, or long threads used to send signals for telephones, televisions, and computers.

Plastic bottles can be ground up and used to fill winter jackets and sleeping bags. Recycled plastic can also be made into boards strong enough to build bridges!

Paper can be recycled into newspaper, writing paper, tissues, cardboard, egg cartons, fruit trays, and even kitty litter!

Now you know where the garbage goes. And you also know that we can all help to save our planet from too much garbage.

What will *you* do to reduce, reuse, and recycle?

a division of
ABRAMS & COMPANY Publishers, Inc.
61 Mattatuck Heights
Waterbury, CT 06705
www.letterpeople.com
1–800–227–9120

Read-to-Me™

Who Will Help Ms. A?
Beautiful Buttons: A Biography of Mr. B
The Clue (Mr. C)
The Dinosaur Detective (Mr. D)
Is It an Earthquake? (Ms. E)
The Fib (Ms. F)
Where Does the Garbage Go? (Mr. G)
The Right Day for a Haircut (Mr. H)
Incredible Insects: A Poetry ANThology (Mr. I)
The Jazz Jamboree (Ms. J)
KABOOM! (Ms. K)
Ha! Ha! Ha! (Ms. L)
The More the Merrier! (Mr. M)
Not Now, Mr. N!
The Opposite Obstacle Course (Mr. O)
The Perfect Pet (Ms. P)
I'm Glad I Asked (Mr. Q)
Real Friends (Mr. R)
A Super Day for Sailing (Ms. S)
Time for a Taxi (Ms. T)
There's No Space Like Home (Ms. U)
Ms. V's Vacation
Weather Watch (Ms. W)
I'm Different (Mr. X)
Just for You (Ms. Y)
Who's New at the Zoo? (Mr. Z)